THE ART OF NOT CARING

Embrace Freedom and Inner Peace

Leah Luthor

ATI Publishing

CONTENTS

Title Page
Introduction   1
Chapter 1   3
Chapter 2   11
Chapter 3   19
Chapter 4   27
Chapter 5   35
Chapter 6   43
Chapter 7   51
Chapter 8   59
Conclusion   67

INTRODUCTION

In a world driven by external validation and the pursuit of perfection, it's easy to find ourselves ensnared in a never-ending cycle of stress and anxiety. We are constantly bombarded with expectations, judgments, and comparisons, causing us to lose sight of our true selves and what truly matters in life.

But what if there was another way of living? A path that leads to liberation, contentment, and genuine inner peace. Welcome to the journey of "The Art of Not Caring."

This book is an exploration of the transformative power of embracing indifference – not as an apathetic withdrawal from the world but as a conscious choice to reclaim our autonomy, happiness, and well-being. It's about stepping away from the heavy burden of others' opinions and societal pressures and finding the courage to define success and happiness on our own terms.

Throughout these pages, we will uncover the illusions that have held us captive, understanding that the desire to control everything is a futile endeavor. We will learn to let go of the shackles of comparison and embrace our unique selves, recognizing the beauty in our imperfections.

"The Art of Not Caring" is not a call to abandon empathy

or compassion. Rather, it's an invitation to cultivate a healthy detachment that allows us to empathize without sacrificing our boundaries and mental well-being. It's about reclaiming our time and energy, so we can invest them in the pursuits that truly align with our passions and values.

Together, we will explore the power of authenticity, self-love, and forgiveness as essential tools in our journey towards freedom. We will discover the art of selective ignorance, navigating the overwhelming noise of the world with mindfulness and purpose.

Ultimately, the aim is not to become indifferent to life's wonders but to let go of what no longer serves us, freeing ourselves from the weight of unnecessary worries and insecurities.

So, whether you are seeking solace in turbulent times or striving for personal growth, join us on this path of self-discovery. Embrace the essence of not caring, and let it guide you towards a life filled with genuine joy, inner peace, and a deeper connection with your true self. The adventure awaits – are you ready to embark on this liberating journey?

CHAPTER 1

Unmasking the Illusion of Control

In the pursuit of happiness and fulfillment, we often find ourselves desperately clinging to the illusion of control. We strive to micromanage every aspect of our lives, believing that if we can orchestrate everything perfectly, we will be shielded from life's uncertainties and hardships. Yet, the more we grasp for control, the more elusive it becomes.

In this chapter, we embark on a profound journey of self-reflection, challenging the deeply ingrained belief that we can control the uncontrollable. We will explore the true nature of control and discover the profound freedom that lies in releasing our grip on life's reigns.

Throughout our lives, we encounter situations that are simply beyond our control – the unpredictable twists of fate, the whims of others, and the ever-changing tides of life. We must confront the truth that no matter how meticulously we plan, life has a way of surprising us, and this realization can be both terrifying and liberating.

By delving into the depths of our desire for control, we will come to understand that it often stems from fear – fear of failure, rejection, or the unknown. We will learn to embrace vulnerability as a gateway to growth and self-discovery, recognizing that surrendering control does not signify weakness but rather strength and resilience.

Through stories of those who have found solace in relinquishing control, we will witness the immense power of acceptance. By acknowledging the limits of our control, we free ourselves from the burden of incessant worrying and allow room for serendipity and new possibilities to unfold.

Moreover, as we explore the concept of adaptability, we will learn that letting go of control does not equate to being passive observers in our own lives. On the contrary, it empowers us to face challenges with flexibility and creativity, adapting to circumstances while maintaining our inner equilibrium.

In this chapter, we embark on a transformative journey toward a deeper understanding of ourselves and the world around us. It is an invitation to release the tight grip we have on life and open ourselves up to the beautiful uncertainty that life has to offer.

So, let us delve into the heart of this chapter, ready to unmask the illusion of control, embrace the wisdom of acceptance, and discover the true meaning of liberation on this extraordinary path of self-discovery and growth.

Letting Go of the Need to Control Every Aspect of Life

In our quest for security and certainty, it is natural to desire control over every aspect of our lives. We create detailed plans, set rigid expectations, and strive to orchestrate every event to unfold exactly as we envision. However, the truth is that life is inherently unpredictable, and trying to control every outcome can lead to stress, anxiety, and a sense of powerlessness when things don't go as planned.

So, how can we begin to let go of the need to control every aspect of life? How do we find the balance between taking charge of our destiny and accepting the flow of life's twists and turns? Let us explore some practical strategies and mindsets that can help us release the grip of excessive control and embrace a more harmonious way of being.

Recognize the Limits of Control
The first step is to acknowledge that there are countless variables in life beyond our influence. From external events to other people's choices, we cannot control everything. Accepting this truth allows us to release the pressure of trying to micromanage every situation.

Cultivate Mindfulness
Practicing mindfulness helps us stay present and centered, even amidst uncertainty. By grounding ourselves in the present moment, we can let go of worries about the future or regrets about the past. Mindfulness enables us to focus on what we can control in the here and now, fostering a sense of calm and clarity.

Embrace Imperfection
Perfectionism often drives the need for control. Embrace the idea that imperfection is a natural part of life. Understand that mistakes and setbacks are opportunities for growth and learning. Allow yourself and others the space to be imperfect without judgment.

Surrender to the Flow of Life
Life is a continuous flow of change, and accepting this flow allows us to let go of the need to control outcomes. Embrace the beauty of spontaneity and serendipity. Trust that even amidst uncertainty, life has a way of unfolding in remarkable ways.

Practice Letting Go
Deliberately practice letting go of control in small, manageable situations. Start by allowing others to take the lead in certain situations or resisting the urge to interfere in someone else's decisions. Gradually, expand your comfort zone and let go of control in more significant aspects of life.

Develop Resilience
Building resilience helps us navigate through unexpected challenges without feeling overwhelmed. Instead of attempting to control outcomes, focus on developing the ability to adapt and bounce back from setbacks. Resilience empowers us to thrive in the face of uncertainty.

Seek Support and Guidance
If the need for control stems from deep-rooted fears or anxieties, consider seeking support from a therapist, counselor, or support group. Professional guidance can help uncover underlying issues and provide tools to manage them effectively.

Emphasize Effort over Outcome
Shift your focus from obsessing over the end result to appreciating the effort you put into your endeavors. Celebrate your dedication and commitment rather than fixating on the uncontrollable outcome.

Letting go of the need to control every aspect of life is a liberating journey that leads to greater peace, freedom, and resilience. By embracing uncertainty and releasing the grip of excessive control, we open ourselves up to the richness of life's experiences. Embrace the art of surrender and find comfort in the knowledge that in letting go, we often discover unexpected paths leading to growth, fulfillment, and profound inner peace.

Understanding the Futility of Worrying about the Uncontrollable

Worrying is a natural human response to uncertainty and the fear of the unknown. However, when we find ourselves excessively worrying about things beyond our control, it becomes a futile and draining exercise that erodes our mental well-being. Understanding the futility of worrying about the uncontrollable is crucial to break free from its grip and cultivate a more peaceful and balanced mindset.

The Nature of the Uncontrollable
Life is riddled with elements beyond our influence. From global events to other people's actions and the passage of time, many aspects of life are simply out of our hands. Recognizing and accepting this fundamental truth is the first step in releasing the burden of unnecessary worry.

Worry vs. Problem-Solving
While concern about future outcomes is natural, excessive worrying offers no productive solution. Distinguishing between constructive problem-solving and futile worry is vital. Instead of expending energy on worry, focus on practical actions for situations that are within your control.

The Imaginary Nature of Worry
Most worries about the future never materialize. Our minds tend to create catastrophic scenarios that rarely come to pass. Realize that worrying is often based on conjecture and fear rather than on tangible evidence.

The Toll on Mental and Physical Health
Worrying about the uncontrollable takes a toll on our mental and physical health. It triggers stress responses that can lead to anxiety, insomnia, headaches, and other health issues. Understanding this negative impact can serve as motivation to break free from the cycle of worry.

Embracing Uncertainty as an Inevitable Part of Life
Life is inherently uncertain, and accepting this uncertainty is essential for our emotional well-being. Embracing the ebb and flow of life allows us to adapt and find strength in the face of unpredictability.

Practicing Mindfulness and Presence
Mindfulness involves being fully present in the here and now. By staying rooted in the present moment, we can reduce anxiety

about the future and avoid ruminating on the past. Mindfulness empowers us to focus on what we can control, providing a sense of peace and clarity.

Cultivating Trust in Yourself and Life
Build trust in yourself and your ability to handle whatever comes your way. Cultivate faith in life's unfolding process, trusting that you have the resilience and strength to navigate challenges when they arise.

Surrendering What You Can't Control
Learn to relinquish control over uncontrollable aspects of life. Surrender does not imply giving up; rather, it signifies acknowledging that some things are beyond our influence and choosing to let go of the emotional burden associated with them.

Understanding the futility of worrying about the uncontrollable liberates us from unnecessary anxiety and stress. By acknowledging the limitations of control and embracing uncertainty as an inevitable part of life, we can find greater peace and contentment. Through mindfulness, trust, and surrender, we can navigate life's uncertainties with grace and resilience. Let go of the futile worry and embrace the present moment, for it is in the present that we find the power to shape our perceptions and responses to life's ever-changing landscape.

Cultivating Resilience and Adaptability
Life is a journey filled with twists and turns, challenges and opportunities. To thrive in this ever-changing landscape, cultivating resilience and adaptability is essential. Resilience enables us to bounce back from setbacks, while adaptability allows us to embrace change and thrive in new circumstances. Together, these traits empower us to navigate through life's uncertainties with strength and grace.

Embrace a Growth Mindset
A growth mindset is the foundation of resilience and adaptability.

It involves viewing challenges as opportunities for learning and growth rather than as insurmountable obstacles. Embrace the belief that abilities and intelligence can be developed through effort and experience.

Reframe Adversity as a Stepping Stone
Instead of seeing adversity as a roadblock, reframe it as a stepping stone toward personal growth. Resilient individuals view challenges as opportunities to become stronger, wiser, and more resourceful.

Develop Emotional Intelligence
Emotional intelligence allows us to understand and manage our emotions effectively. By recognizing our feelings, we can respond to difficult situations with composure and make well-informed decisions.

Build a Support System
Having a strong support system of friends, family, or a community can provide valuable encouragement and understanding during tough times. Seek support and be willing to lend support to others as well.

Practice Self-Compassion
Treat yourself with kindness and compassion during challenging times. Acknowledge that everyone faces setbacks and that it's okay to experience difficult emotions. Be gentle with yourself as you navigate through life's ups and downs.

Learn from Adversity
Every challenging situation offers a valuable lesson. Take the time to reflect on past experiences, identify areas for growth, and apply those lessons to future endeavors.

Be Open to Change
Embrace change as an inherent part of life. The ability to adapt and flow with life's changes is crucial for maintaining resilience and well-being. Be open to new experiences and ideas.

Practice Flexibility and Problem-Solving
Approach problems with a flexible mindset, exploring multiple solutions. Adaptability involves being open to alternative approaches when facing obstacles.

Stay Present and Mindful
Mindfulness cultivates presence and awareness, allowing us to stay focused on the present moment rather than ruminating on the past or worrying about the future. Being present helps us adapt to changing circumstances more effectively.

Celebrate Progress, Not Perfection
Celebrate small victories along the way, recognizing that progress is more valuable than perfection. Acknowledge your efforts and accomplishments, even when the outcome may not match your initial expectations.

Cultivating resilience and adaptability is a lifelong journey of self-discovery and growth. By embracing a growth mindset, reframing adversity, developing emotional intelligence, and staying present, we empower ourselves to navigate life's challenges with strength and grace. Embrace change, be open to new experiences, and remember to be kind to yourself along the way. As you cultivate resilience and adaptability, you will discover the remarkable power within you to thrive amidst life's ever-changing landscape.

CHAPTER 2

Redefining Success and Failure

In a world that often measures success by external achievements and societal standards, it is easy to fall into the trap of defining our self-worth solely based on accomplishments. Likewise, failure is commonly perceived as a devastating setback rather than an inevitable part of growth and learning. In this chapter, we embark on a transformative journey of redefining success and failure, freeing ourselves from limiting definitions and embracing a more empowering perspective.

As we dive into this exploration, we challenge the conventional notion that success is synonymous with material wealth, prestigious titles, or widespread recognition. We will discover that true success lies in the alignment between our actions and our core values, finding fulfillment in the pursuit of meaningful goals.

Simultaneously, we'll confront the stigma surrounding failure and embrace it as an invaluable teacher that propels us forward on the path of self-improvement. Instead of viewing failure as a reflection of inadequacy, we'll uncover the wisdom it offers, guiding us to refine our approach and develop resilience.

Through inspiring stories of individuals who have redefined

success and embraced failure, we'll witness the profound transformations that occur when we release the burden of external expectations and nurture our authentic selves.

Together, we will explore the significance of self-compassion and self-awareness in the process of redefining success and failure. By understanding our strengths, weaknesses, and intrinsic motivations, we can craft a personal definition of success that resonates deeply within us.

Furthermore, we'll celebrate the journey itself, recognizing that the pursuit of growth and self-discovery is a victory in its own right. As we redefine success and failure, we shift our focus from comparing ourselves to others to celebrating our individual progress and unique path.

Ultimately, this chapter is an invitation to reclaim our autonomy in shaping our definition of success and to embrace failure as a stepping stone to growth. By doing so, we liberate ourselves from the constraints of societal norms and create space for genuine fulfillment and personal development.

So, let us begin this chapter with an open heart and an open mind, ready to challenge preconceived notions and embrace a more holistic and empowering understanding of success and failure. In doing so, we embark on a journey of self-empowerment, authenticity, and a deeper connection with our true selves.

The Power of Redefining Success on Your Own Terms

In a world heavily influenced by external standards and societal expectations, the concept of success often becomes narrowly defined, leaving little room for individuality and personal fulfillment. However, the power of redefining success on your own terms is a liberating force that allows you to embrace your unique journey and authentic desires. By breaking free from the constraints of external validation, you can craft a meaningful and fulfilling path that aligns with your values and passions.

Embracing Individuality and Authenticity
Redefining success starts with embracing your individuality. Recognize that each person's journey is unique, and there is no one-size-fits-all definition of success. Embrace your authentic self, honoring your passions, interests, and values as the guiding compass on your path to success.

Clarifying Personal Values and Priorities
Take the time to reflect on your core values and what truly matters to you. Define what success means to you beyond material wealth or societal acclaim. Whether it's fostering meaningful relationships, making a positive impact, or pursuing personal growth, let your values guide your vision of success.

Shifting the Focus from Outcomes to Effort
Redefining success involves shifting the emphasis from outcome-based achievements to the effort and dedication you invest in your pursuits. Celebrate the progress you make and the lessons you learn along the way, regardless of the final outcome.

Cultivating Self-Compassion
Embrace self-compassion in your pursuit of success. Recognize that setbacks and challenges are part of any journey and treat yourself with kindness and understanding. Allow room for growth and acknowledge that failure is not a reflection of your worth.

Setting Realistic and Personalized Goals
Set goals that are both challenging and realistic, tailored to your individual aspirations and capabilities. Avoid comparing your progress to others, as each person's journey unfolds at its own pace.

Embracing a Holistic Perspective
Redefining success involves adopting a more holistic perspective

that encompasses various aspects of life. Consider not only professional achievements but also personal growth, well-being, and the quality of relationships in your definition of success.

Creating a Flexible Path
Be open to detours and unexpected opportunities on your path to success. A flexible mindset allows you to adapt and seize new possibilities that may lead to unforeseen, yet deeply fulfilling, experiences.

Celebrating Your Progress
Celebrate your achievements, no matter how small or incremental they may seem. Acknowledge the effort you invest and the resilience you demonstrate along the way. Each step forward is a testament to your commitment to personal growth.

The power of redefining success on your own terms lies in embracing your unique identity and crafting a meaningful life journey aligned with your values and passions. By breaking free from the confines of external expectations, you can embrace personal growth, self-compassion, and fulfillment. As you set your sights on success that is authentic to you, remember that the journey is a continuous process of learning, evolving, and celebrating the progress made. Embrace the empowering journey of self-discovery and create a life filled with purpose, joy, and a deeper connection with your true self.

Embracing Failure as a Stepping Stone to Growth

Failure—the very word can evoke feelings of disappointment, shame, and defeat. Yet, what if we could shift our perspective and see failure not as a dead-end but as a stepping stone on the path to growth and self-discovery? Embracing failure as a powerful catalyst for personal development can transform the way we navigate challenges and setbacks in life.

Redefining Failure
Failure is not a reflection of our worth as individuals but rather

a natural part of the learning process. It's an opportunity to gain insights, refine our strategies, and develop the resilience needed to succeed in the long run.

Embracing the Growth Mindset
The growth mindset, as coined by psychologist Carol Dweck, is the belief that our abilities and intelligence can be developed through dedication and hard work. By adopting a growth mindset, we view failure as a chance to learn and improve rather than a fixed limitation.

Learning from Setbacks
Each failure provides valuable lessons and feedback. Take the time to reflect on what went wrong, what could be done differently, and what insights can be applied to future endeavors. Use failures as stepping stones to make informed decisions and progress.

Building Resilience and Perseverance
Embracing failure builds resilience—the ability to bounce back from adversity. It strengthens our determination, helping us persevere in the face of challenges and setbacks. With each failure, we become more equipped to tackle future obstacles.

Embracing Creativity and Innovation
Failure encourages us to think outside the box and explore new solutions. It sparks creativity and innovation as we seek alternative paths to success. Some of history's greatest innovations arose from the willingness to learn from failure.

Letting Go of Fear
Fear of failure can paralyze us and prevent us from taking risks. By embracing failure, we release the fear that holds us back and become more willing to embrace new opportunities and challenges.

Overcoming Limiting Beliefs
Failures often reveal the limiting beliefs that hinder our progress. Embracing failure allows us to confront these beliefs head-on and

challenge their validity. By overcoming these barriers, we open ourselves up to new possibilities and growth.

Celebrating Effort and Progress
Rather than solely focusing on the outcome, celebrate the effort and progress made in the face of challenges. Acknowledge the courage it took to try, the resilience shown in overcoming obstacles, and the commitment to personal growth.

Embracing failure as a stepping stone to growth empowers us to shift our mindset and transform setbacks into powerful opportunities for learning and self-improvement. By viewing failure through the lens of the growth mindset, we cultivate resilience, creativity, and perseverance. Embrace failure as a valuable teacher that propels you forward on the journey of personal development. As you embrace the transformative power of failure, you'll discover the strength to face challenges with courage and the wisdom to turn obstacles into stepping stones toward growth and success.

Recognizing the Importance of Self-Compassion in the Face of Setbacks

Setbacks are an inevitable part of life's journey. Whether it's a personal or professional disappointment, facing failure can be challenging and emotionally taxing. In these moments, the significance of self-compassion becomes paramount. Practicing self-compassion is a powerful tool for navigating setbacks with grace, resilience, and emotional well-being.

Embracing Imperfection
Self-compassion starts with recognizing that everyone faces setbacks and that imperfection is a natural aspect of being human. Instead of being self-critical, embrace the idea that experiencing setbacks is a shared human experience.

Responding with Kindness

Be gentle and understanding with yourself during difficult times. Treat yourself as you would treat a dear friend facing a similar setback. Extend compassion and kindness to yourself, offering the same support and encouragement you would offer to others.

Avoiding Self-Judgment

Self-compassion involves avoiding harsh self-judgment and self-criticism. Refrain from blaming yourself or engaging in negative self-talk. Instead, remind yourself that setbacks are opportunities for growth and learning.

Validating Emotions

Recognize and validate your emotions in the face of setbacks. Allow yourself to experience feelings of disappointment, frustration, or sadness without judgment. Acknowledge that it is okay to feel and process these emotions.

Practicing Mindfulness

Mindfulness cultivates presence and non-judgmental awareness of your thoughts and emotions. By practicing mindfulness, you can observe your feelings without becoming overwhelmed by them. Mindfulness helps you respond to setbacks with greater clarity and composure.

Learning from Setbacks

View setbacks as valuable learning experiences rather than failures. Identify the lessons and insights that can be gained from the experience. Understand that setbacks provide opportunities for personal growth and development.

Treating Yourself with Patience

Healing and recovering from setbacks take time. Be patient with yourself and allow yourself the space to process emotions and recover at your own pace. Avoid putting pressure on yourself to bounce back immediately.

Maintaining Perspective

In the face of setbacks, try to maintain perspective and avoid catastrophizing the situation. Remind yourself that setbacks are temporary and do not define your worth or potential.

The importance of self-compassion in the face of setbacks cannot be overstated. By embracing imperfection, responding with kindness, and avoiding self-judgment, you create a nurturing environment for emotional healing and growth. Self-compassion helps you navigate setbacks with resilience, maintaining a balanced perspective and allowing yourself the space to learn and evolve from challenges. As you cultivate self-compassion, you'll find the strength to face setbacks with grace, empowering yourself to move forward with renewed determination and a deeper sense of self-awareness and inner peace.

CHAPTER 3

Embracing Authenticity

In a world filled with pressures to conform and meet societal expectations, the journey to discovering and embracing our authentic selves can be both challenging and liberating. Embracing authenticity is about daring to show up as our true selves, free from the masks of pretense and societal roles. It's about honoring our unique identity and expressing it with courage and vulnerability.

This chapter delves into the profound significance of embracing authenticity and the transformative impact it can have on our lives. We explore the rewards of living in alignment with our core values, passions, and beliefs, and the courage it takes to defy societal norms that may not align with our authentic selves.

Throughout these pages, we embark on a journey of self-exploration and self-acceptance. We delve into the power of vulnerability, recognizing that authenticity often requires us to expose our true feelings and thoughts without fear of judgment. In doing so, we forge deeper connections with others and ourselves.

Moreover, we confront the fear of rejection and the discomfort of stepping out of our comfort zones to reveal our authentic selves.

We learn that by embracing authenticity, we attract like-minded individuals and foster more meaningful relationships built on genuine connections.

As we journey through the chapters, we celebrate the beauty in our imperfections, knowing that authenticity is not about being flawless but about embracing our unique qualities and quirks. We discover that it is okay to be vulnerable, as vulnerability is the birthplace of true connection and empathy.

Throughout the stories of individuals who have embarked on the path of authenticity, we gain insight into the power of shedding societal expectations and finding strength in our authentic voices. We uncover the joy and fulfillment that comes from living a life in alignment with our true selves.

So, let us embark on this chapter with open hearts and minds, ready to embrace the power of authenticity. Let us dare to be true to ourselves, free from the shackles of external validation, and step into the fullness of who we are. As we journey toward authenticity, we discover the courage to live life on our terms, celebrating our uniqueness, and nurturing a profound sense of self-love and acceptance.

The Art of Being Unapologetically Yourself

Authenticity is a precious gift we can give to ourselves and the world. It's about living in harmony with our true selves, free from the constraints of external expectations. Embracing the art of being unapologetically yourself is a courageous and transformative journey that invites us to celebrate our uniqueness and honor the voice within.

Embrace Your Uniqueness
Each of us is a tapestry of experiences, beliefs, and passions that make us beautifully unique. Embrace your individuality and celebrate the qualities that set you apart from others. Recognize that your uniqueness is a valuable asset, and the world is richer for

having you in it.

Shed the Masks of Pretense
Let go of the masks you wear to conform to societal expectations. Embrace vulnerability and be unafraid to reveal your authentic self. By shedding pretense, you allow yourself to connect with others on a deeper level and create meaningful relationships based on genuineness.

Defy External Validation
Relying on external validation can be a trap that stifles authenticity. Free yourself from the need for approval from others, recognizing that your self-worth is not determined by others' opinions. Validate yourself based on your values, passions, and intrinsic worth.

Embrace Vulnerability and Courage
Being unapologetically yourself requires courage. Embrace vulnerability as the pathway to genuine connection and growth. Be brave enough to share your authentic voice and stand firm in your truth, even when it feels uncomfortable.

Let Go of Perfectionism
Perfectionism can be a roadblock to authenticity. Release the burden of striving for flawlessness and embrace the beauty of imperfection. Allow yourself to make mistakes and learn from them, knowing that they are stepping stones to growth.

Set Boundaries
Protect your authenticity by setting healthy boundaries with others. Be unapologetic about honoring your needs, values, and personal space. Boundaries create a safe space for you to express yourself authentically.

Practice Self-Compassion
Be kind and compassionate to yourself as you embark on this journey of authenticity. Embrace self-compassion as a guiding force that supports you through setbacks and challenges. Treat

yourself with the same understanding and care you would offer to a dear friend.

Cultivate Self-Awareness
Deepen your self-awareness to better understand your values, beliefs, and desires. Self-awareness helps you navigate life in alignment with your authentic self and make choices that resonate with who you truly are.

The art of being unapologetically yourself is an empowering journey of self-discovery, self-acceptance, and self-expression. Embrace your uniqueness, shed the masks of pretense, and defy external validation to live authentically. By embracing vulnerability, courage, and self-compassion, you cultivate a profound connection with yourself and others. Embrace your imperfections, set boundaries, and cultivate self-awareness to live a life that honors the fullness of who you are. Remember, you are worthy of love, acceptance, and celebration, just as you are. Embrace the art of being unapologetically yourself and witness the transformative power it brings to your life and the world around you.

Overcoming the Fear of Judgment and Rejection

The fear of judgment and rejection can be paralyzing, preventing us from fully embracing our authentic selves and pursuing our dreams. It's a natural human instinct to seek acceptance and approval from others, but when this fear becomes overwhelming, it can hinder personal growth and limit life's possibilities. Overcoming the fear of judgment and rejection is a powerful journey of self-liberation and empowerment.

Recognize the Source of Fear
Understanding the root cause of your fear is the first step in overcoming it. Reflect on past experiences or conditioning that may have contributed to the fear of judgment and rejection. Recognize that these fears often stem from our desire to be liked

and valued by others.

Challenge Negative Self-Talk

The fear of judgment often leads to negative self-talk and self-doubt. Challenge these thoughts and replace them with positive affirmations and self-encouragement. Remember that you are worthy and deserving of love and acceptance, regardless of others' opinions.

Embrace Vulnerability

Embracing vulnerability is an essential aspect of overcoming the fear of judgment and rejection. Recognize that vulnerability is a strength, not a weakness. By allowing yourself to be vulnerable, you open the door to genuine connections and authentic relationships.

Reframe Rejection as Learning Opportunities

Shift your perspective on rejection. Instead of viewing it as a personal failure, reframe rejection as an opportunity to learn and grow. Every rejection can provide valuable feedback and insights that can guide you toward improvement and new possibilities.

Focus on Self-Approval

Seeking validation from others can be a never-ending pursuit. Redirect your focus inward and prioritize self-approval. Trust your instincts, honor your values, and make decisions aligned with your authentic self.

Surround Yourself with Supportive People

Surround yourself with individuals who uplift and support you. Seek out friends, family, or communities that celebrate your authenticity and encourage your personal growth. Positive influences can help counteract the fear of judgment and rejection.

Set Boundaries

Establishing healthy boundaries is crucial in overcoming the fear of judgment and rejection. Set limits on the amount of influence others have on your self-worth and decision-making process.

Protect your mental and emotional well-being by defining what you will and will not tolerate from others.

Practice Self-Compassion
Be compassionate with yourself as you navigate the fear of judgment and rejection. Treat yourself with kindness and understanding during challenging times. Acknowledge that facing these fears is a courageous step toward personal growth.

Overcoming the fear of judgment and rejection is a transformative journey that liberates us from the limitations imposed by external opinions. By recognizing the source of fear, challenging negative self-talk, and embracing vulnerability, we unlock the power to embrace our authentic selves fully. Reframing rejection, focusing on self-approval, and surrounding ourselves with supportive individuals empowers us to navigate through life's challenges with resilience and self-assurance. As we cultivate self-compassion and set healthy boundaries, we create a safe space to flourish authentically. Embrace this journey of empowerment, for within it lies the key to living a life that is true to yourself and free from the fear of judgment and rejection.

Fostering Genuine Connections by Being Authentic

Authenticity is the cornerstone of genuine connections with others. When we show up as our true selves, unapologetically and vulnerably, we create a space for authentic relationships to blossom. Fostering genuine connections by being authentic not only enriches our lives but also allows us to form meaningful bonds with those around us.

Embracing Vulnerability
Vulnerability is the gateway to genuine connections. By embracing vulnerability, we allow others to see our true selves, complete with imperfections and insecurities. This openness creates an atmosphere of trust and intimacy that strengthens

relationships.

Letting Go of Masks and Pretense
Release the need to wear masks or pretend to be someone you are not. Authentic connections thrive when we drop the façade and show up as our genuine selves. Let others see the real you, and in turn, encourage them to do the same.

Active Listening and Empathy
To foster genuine connections, practice active listening and empathy. Pay attention to what others are saying, and seek to understand their thoughts and feelings. Show empathy and support, making others feel valued and heard.

Honoring Your Boundaries
Authentic connections are built on mutual respect and consideration of each other's boundaries. Be clear about your boundaries and communicate them openly and honestly. Likewise, respect the boundaries of others to create a safe and respectful environment.

Celebrating Individuality
Appreciate and celebrate the individuality of others. Authentic connections thrive when we embrace and value the uniqueness of each person. Avoid judgment or comparison and instead, celebrate the diverse qualities that make each individual special.

Sharing Your Truths and Values
Be open about your beliefs, passions, and values. Sharing your truths with others allows for a deeper understanding of your authentic self. When you express your core values, you attract like-minded individuals and create stronger connections based on shared beliefs.

Accepting Imperfection
Authentic connections are not about perfection; they are about embracing imperfection. Accept that both you and others are human, and no one is without flaws. Embrace the beauty in

imperfection and foster an environment of acceptance.

Prioritizing Quality Over Quantity
Authentic connections are not about having an extensive network of acquaintances but rather meaningful relationships with a few people who truly understand and accept you. Prioritize quality over quantity, investing time and effort in fostering deeper connections.

Fostering genuine connections by being authentic is a transformative practice that enriches our lives with meaningful relationships. Embrace vulnerability, let go of pretense, and listen empathetically to others. Honor your boundaries, celebrate individuality, and share your truths and values with courage. Accept imperfection and prioritize quality connections. By being authentic, you create a space for others to be authentic as well, fostering a network of relationships built on trust, mutual understanding, and respect. As you embrace authenticity and cultivate genuine connections, you'll experience the profound beauty of building meaningful bonds that stand the test of time and bring joy and fulfillment to your life and the lives of those around you.

CHAPTER 4

Escaping the Comparison Trap

In a world inundated with social media and constant exposure to the lives of others, the comparison trap has become an all-too-common pitfall. The temptation to measure ourselves against others—whether it's their achievements, possessions, or appearance—can lead to feelings of inadequacy and self-doubt. Escaping the comparison trap is a transformative journey that liberates us from the shackles of constant comparison and allows us to embrace our unique path with confidence and self-assurance.

In this chapter, we delve into the pervasive nature of the comparison trap and the profound impact it can have on our mental and emotional well-being. We explore the consequences of comparing ourselves to others and the toll it takes on our self-esteem and happiness.

As we journey through these pages, we uncover the root causes of the comparison trap and how societal pressures and unrealistic standards perpetuate this cycle. We recognize that comparing ourselves to others robs us of the joy of our own accomplishments and hinders our ability to fully appreciate our unique strengths.

Throughout this chapter, we challenge the fallacy of one-size-fits-all success and explore the dangers of seeking validation solely through external comparisons. By breaking free from the comparison trap, we reclaim our autonomy in defining our self-worth and pave the way for genuine self-acceptance and self-love.

Moreover, we delve into the power of cultivating gratitude and self-compassion as antidotes to the comparison trap. By focusing on our own journey and embracing our individuality, we empower ourselves to overcome feelings of inadequacy and embrace a healthier perspective.

As we learn from the stories of individuals who have escaped the comparison trap, we gain insight into the transformative impact of embracing our unique qualities and pursuing our passions without comparison to others. We discover the freedom that comes from living life on our terms, free from the burden of constant comparison.

So, let us embark on this chapter with open hearts and minds, ready to liberate ourselves from the comparison trap. Let us embrace the beauty of our individual journey and celebrate the progress we make on our own terms. By escaping the comparison trap, we unlock the door to a life filled with authenticity, self-love, and a deeper connection with our true selves.

Understanding the Harm of Constant Comparison

In today's hyper-connected world, constant comparison has become an ever-present and insidious challenge that can wreak havoc on our mental and emotional well-being. While it's natural for humans to assess themselves in relation to others, the constant exposure to social media, peer pressure, and societal expectations exacerbates the harmful effects of comparison.

Erosion of Self-Esteem
Constantly comparing ourselves to others can erode our self-esteem and self-worth. When we focus on what we lack compared to others, we diminish the value of our own accomplishments and

unique qualities.

Cultivation of Inadequacy
Comparison often leads to feelings of inadequacy and a sense of not measuring up. This can create a vicious cycle of self-doubt and dissatisfaction, preventing us from fully appreciating our own journey.

Missed Opportunities for Growth
When we fixate on what others have achieved or attained, we may neglect our own growth and potential. The comparison trap can blind us to opportunities for personal development and pursuing our passions.

Strain on Relationships
Constant comparison can lead to envy and jealousy, causing strain on our relationships with others. It may lead to feelings of competition, which can overshadow genuine connections and shared experiences.

Diminished Authenticity
Comparison often fosters a desire to conform to societal norms or the expectations of others. In doing so, we may sacrifice our authenticity and true selves, leading to a loss of personal fulfillment.

Negative Impact on Mental Health
The constant pursuit of measuring up to others can contribute to increased stress, anxiety, and even depression. It puts immense pressure on our mental health and well-being.

Inequality of Comparison
Comparison is often unfair as we tend to compare our weaknesses to others' strengths. This skewed perception can leave us feeling inadequate and discouraged.

Distracted from Personal Goals
The preoccupation with others' lives and achievements can distract us from focusing on our own goals and aspirations. This

distraction hinders our progress and fulfillment.

Disconnect from Gratitude
Comparison can overshadow gratitude for our own blessings and achievements. By constantly seeking what others have, we may lose sight of the abundance in our own lives.

Limited Joy in Life
Constantly comparing ourselves to others robs us of the joy of being content with who we are and what we have. It prevents us from savoring the present and finding happiness in our own unique journey.

Understanding the harm of constant comparison is crucial in breaking free from the comparison trap. By recognizing how comparison affects our self-esteem, relationships, and mental health, we empower ourselves to shift our perspective and embrace self-acceptance. By nurturing gratitude, self-compassion, and a focus on personal growth, we can liberate ourselves from the harmful effects of constant comparison. Let us choose authenticity over conformity, celebrate our individual journey, and cultivate a healthier and more fulfilling way of relating to ourselves and others.

Embracing Uniqueness and Celebrating Diversity

The beauty of humanity lies in its diversity—our unique backgrounds, perspectives, and experiences shape a rich tapestry that weaves together the fabric of society. Embracing uniqueness and celebrating diversity is not only a powerful testament to the beauty of human existence but also a transformative practice that fosters unity, understanding, and a sense of belonging.

Honoring Individuality
Each person is a masterpiece, intricately shaped by their experiences and choices. Embrace your individuality and recognize that being different is what makes you extraordinary. Celebrate the qualities that make you unique and honor the same

in others.

Cultivating Empathy
By celebrating diversity, we cultivate empathy and understanding. Taking the time to learn about others' experiences and perspectives helps us build bridges of compassion, fostering a deeper sense of connection.

Creating an Inclusive Environment
Embracing uniqueness means creating an inclusive environment where everyone feels welcome and valued. Celebrate diversity by encouraging diverse voices and perspectives to be heard and respected.

Breaking Down Stereotypes
Stereotypes often arise from ignorance and generalizations. Celebrating diversity involves challenging stereotypes and seeking to understand people as individuals rather than as representatives of a group.

Embracing Cross-Cultural Learning
Explore and appreciate different cultures, traditions, and customs. Embrace the opportunity to learn from others and celebrate the richness that cultural diversity brings to our lives.

Fostering Collaboration and Innovation
Diverse perspectives contribute to more comprehensive problem-solving and innovative solutions. Embracing uniqueness fosters an environment where collaboration thrives, leading to greater creativity and progress.

Promoting Social Harmony
By celebrating diversity, we build a society that is more harmonious and inclusive. This inclusivity promotes unity and understanding, reducing the barriers that divide us.

Encouraging Personal Growth
Engaging with diverse perspectives and experiences opens our minds to new ideas and broadens our horizons. Embracing

uniqueness encourages personal growth, making us more open-minded and compassionate individuals.

Leading by Example
Celebrate your own uniqueness, and others will follow suit. Be an advocate for diversity and inclusion, leading by example to create a more accepting and diverse community.

Embracing Unity in Diversity
Celebrating diversity does not mean erasing differences but rather acknowledging them while finding common ground. Embrace unity in diversity, cherishing the beauty of our varied experiences while recognizing our shared humanity.

Embracing uniqueness and celebrating diversity is a powerful practice that elevates humanity to its highest potential. By honoring individuality, cultivating empathy, and promoting inclusivity, we build a society that thrives on compassion, understanding, and unity. Let us break down barriers, challenge stereotypes, and foster collaboration among diverse voices. Embrace the richness that comes from engaging with different cultures and perspectives. As we celebrate diversity, we unlock the transformative power of acceptance and create a world that cherishes the uniqueness of every individual, united by the thread of our shared humanity.

Practicing Gratitude and Finding Contentment in What You Have

In a world that often urges us to constantly strive for more, the practice of gratitude and contentment becomes a powerful antidote to the ever-present desire for accumulation. Cultivating gratitude is a transformative journey that shifts our focus from what we lack to what we already possess, fostering a deep sense of appreciation and fulfillment in our lives.

Embracing the Power of Gratitude

Practicing gratitude involves recognizing and acknowledging the blessings, experiences, and people we are thankful for. It is about finding joy in the present moment and expressing heartfelt thanks for the abundance surrounding us.

Finding Beauty in Simplicity

Contentment arises when we find beauty and happiness in life's simple pleasures. It could be the warmth of a sunny day, the aroma of freshly brewed coffee, or a heartfelt conversation with a friend. These everyday moments become a source of contentment when we pause to appreciate them.

Shifting from Scarcity to Abundance

Gratitude liberates us from the clutches of scarcity mentality, the belief that there is never enough. By focusing on what we have rather than what we lack, we open ourselves to a world of abundance and possibility.

Letting Go of Comparison

Comparing ourselves to others is a trap that robs us of contentment. When we cultivate gratitude, we shift our attention from what others possess to the unique blessings that grace our own lives.

Appreciating Life's Simple Joys

Contentment is not found in grand achievements or material possessions, but in appreciating the little joys that color our daily lives. By finding delight in these small moments, we enrich our overall sense of fulfillment.

Cultivating Mindfulness

Practicing gratitude encourages mindfulness, being fully present and aware of the beauty and goodness that surrounds us. It allows us to slow down, savor the present, and find contentment in the now.

Nurturing Positivity and Resilience

Gratitude fosters a positive outlook, enabling us to navigate challenges with resilience and hope. When we are content with what we have, we become better equipped to face life's uncertainties with grace.

Strengthening Relationships
Expressing gratitude to others enhances our relationships and creates deeper connections. Acknowledging the impact of loved ones in our lives fosters a sense of belonging and strengthens bonds.

Finding Joy in Giving
Contentment flourishes when we practice generosity and give back to others. The act of giving, whether through kindness, support, or charity, nurtures a sense of purpose and fulfillment.

Fostering Inner Peace
Gratitude and contentment go hand in hand with inner peace. By appreciating the richness of our lives, we release the restlessness that comes from always wanting more.

Practicing gratitude and finding contentment in what we have is a journey of self-discovery and mindfulness. It empowers us to shift our focus from the pursuit of more to the celebration of what already enriches our lives. By embracing the simple joys, nurturing positivity, and expressing thanks, we unlock the door to a deeper sense of fulfillment and a more meaningful connection with the world around us. As we walk this path of gratitude, we find that contentment lies not in chasing after abundance but in cherishing the abundance that already resides within and around us.

CHAPTER 5

Mastering the Art of Selective Ignorance

In a world flooded with information, opinions, and distractions, mastering the art of selective ignorance becomes a powerful skill for navigating the complexities of modern life. Selective ignorance is not about being uninformed or ignorant in general, but rather about consciously choosing what to pay attention to and what to filter out. It is a strategic practice that allows us to preserve our mental clarity, focus, and well-being amidst the constant barrage of information overload.

This chapter explores the significance of selective ignorance and its transformative impact on our lives. We delve into the concept of information filtering and how it enables us to stay in control of our attention and energy. By mastering the art of selective ignorance, we create space for more meaningful experiences, deeper connections, and a heightened sense of presence.

Throughout these pages, we examine the detrimental effects of information overload and how it can lead to decision fatigue, reduced productivity, and increased stress. We uncover the wisdom of tuning out irrelevant noise and cultivating a purposeful and mindful engagement with the world.

Moreover, we explore the art of saying "no" to distractions and commitments that do not align with our values and goals. By doing so, we reclaim our time and energy, channeling them toward activities that nurture our passions and foster personal growth.

As we journey through this chapter, we learn the importance of setting boundaries and protecting our mental space. We discover that by being selective about what we consume, whether it's media, social interactions, or information, we safeguard our emotional well-being and cultivate a more intentional and balanced lifestyle.

In addition, we explore the intersection of selective ignorance with self-awareness, focus, and creativity. By fine-tuning our attention, we enhance our ability to engage deeply with our passions, thoughts, and ideas, unlocking new levels of innovation and insight.

So, let us embark on this chapter with open minds and hearts, ready to embrace the art of selective ignorance. Let us become intentional curators of our own experiences, seeking clarity, purpose, and authenticity. By mastering the art of selective ignorance, we gain the freedom to shape our own narrative, finding meaning amidst the noise, and fostering a profound sense of empowerment and fulfillment.

Identifying and Eliminating Toxic Influences in Your Life

Our journey through life is profoundly impacted by the company we keep and the influences we allow into our lives. Toxic influences, whether they are people, habits, or environments, can drain our energy, hinder our growth, and erode our well-being. Identifying and eliminating toxic influences is a courageous and transformative act of self-preservation and self-empowerment.

Recognizing Toxic Influences
The first step in freeing ourselves from toxic influences is to recognize them. Be attentive to how certain people or situations make you feel. Notice patterns of negativity, manipulation, or constant drama that drain your energy and happiness.

Trusting Your Intuition
Your intuition is a powerful guide in identifying toxic influences. If something or someone doesn't feel right, trust that inner voice. It may be trying to protect you from harm or steer you toward healthier choices.

Assessing Relationships
Evaluate your relationships honestly. Are there individuals who consistently bring you down or undermine your self-worth? If so, consider whether these connections are worth preserving or if it's time to distance yourself.

Setting Boundaries
Establish clear boundaries to protect yourself from toxic influences. Be assertive in communicating your limits and avoiding situations that compromise your well-being.

Redefining Your Circle
Surround yourself with positive and supportive individuals who uplift and inspire you. Prioritize relationships that nurture your growth and well-being, and let go of those that hinder your progress.

Breaking Free from Negative Habits
Identify negative habits that perpetuate toxic influences in your life. Whether it's excessive social media use, self-destructive behaviors, or unhealthy coping mechanisms, work towards breaking free from these patterns.

Creating a Positive Environment
Cultivate a positive environment that fosters your personal growth and happiness. Surround yourself with uplifting

influences, such as books, podcasts, or activities that align with your values and aspirations.

Practicing Self-Care
Nurturing yourself is essential in eliminating toxic influences. Engage in self-care practices that replenish your energy and promote emotional well-being, such as mindfulness, exercise, or spending time in nature.

Seeking Professional Help if Needed
In some cases, toxic influences can have a profound impact on our mental and emotional health. If you find it challenging to cope or break free from harmful situations, don't hesitate to seek support from a therapist or counselor.

10. Embracing Empowerment
Recognize that identifying and eliminating toxic influences is an empowering act of self-love and self-respect. Taking charge of your environment and relationships allows you to create a life that is authentic, fulfilling, and free from negativity.

Identifying and eliminating toxic influences in your life is a transformative process that liberates you from draining and harmful energies. Trust your intuition, set boundaries, and surround yourself with positive influences that nurture your growth and well-being. By prioritizing self-care and self-empowerment, you create a life that reflects your authentic self, enabling you to flourish and thrive on your journey toward happiness and fulfillment. Remember, you have the power to curate your own experiences and shape a life that aligns with your true values and aspirations.

Setting Healthy Boundaries to Protect Your Well-Being

Healthy boundaries are essential for safeguarding your mental, emotional, and physical well-being. They define the limits of what you are comfortable with and establish a framework for how you want to be treated. Setting healthy boundaries is a transformative practice that empowers you to take charge of your life, preserve your energy, and foster healthier relationships.

Recognizing the Importance of Boundaries
Understand that setting boundaries is not selfish; it is an act of self-respect and self-care. Healthy boundaries help you maintain a sense of balance, prevent burnout, and protect your overall well-being.

Identifying Your Limits
Take time to identify your limits and needs. Reflect on what makes you feel uncomfortable or drained in various situations, whether it's at work, in relationships, or during social interactions.

Communicating Assertively
Effectively communicate your boundaries with clarity and assertiveness. Be direct and honest when expressing what you are comfortable with and what you are not.

Learning to Say No
Saying "no" is a powerful tool in setting boundaries. Don't feel obligated to agree to everything; it's okay to decline requests or invitations that don't align with your priorities or values.

Trusting Your Instincts
Trust your instincts when it comes to recognizing situations or people that may violate your boundaries. If something feels off or uncomfortable, listen to that inner voice and take action accordingly.

Setting Boundaries in Relationships
Boundaries are crucial in all types of relationships. Communicate your needs and expectations with your partner, family, and friends to foster healthier and more respectful connections.

Avoiding Overcommitment

Be mindful of your commitments and avoid overextending yourself. Prioritize your well-being and make sure to leave enough time for rest and activities that bring you joy.

Practicing Self-Compassion
Setting boundaries may sometimes evoke guilt or fear of disappointing others. Practice self-compassion and remind yourself that taking care of yourself is a priority.

Adjusting Boundaries as Needed
Your boundaries may evolve over time, and that's okay. Be open to adjusting them as needed, depending on the circumstances and your personal growth.

Seeking Support
If setting boundaries feels challenging, seek support from a therapist, counselor, or support group. Professional guidance can help you navigate through the process and build healthier boundary-setting skills.

Setting healthy boundaries is a transformative practice that empowers you to protect your well-being, cultivate healthier relationships, and lead a more fulfilling life. By recognizing the importance of boundaries, identifying your limits, and communicating assertively, you create a space where you can thrive and grow. Trust your instincts, practice self-compassion, and remember that it's okay to say no and prioritize your needs. Embrace the power of setting healthy boundaries, and you'll discover newfound strength, self-respect, and a greater sense of balance and fulfillment in your life.

Navigating Social Media and Information Overload Mindfully

In the age of technology and interconnectedness, social media and the influx of information have become integral parts of our daily lives. While these tools offer unprecedented opportunities for communication and knowledge sharing, they also present challenges, including information overload and the potential for mindless consumption. Navigating social media and information overload mindfully is a transformative practice that enables us to harness the benefits of these platforms while preserving our mental clarity and well-being.

Understanding Information Overload
Information overload occurs when we are exposed to an excessive amount of information, leading to feelings of overwhelm and difficulty in processing and prioritizing what truly matters.

Awareness of Social Media Impact
Be aware of how social media influences your thoughts, emotions, and behaviors. Mindfully observe how you feel after spending time on these platforms and adjust your usage accordingly.

Setting Intentions for Social Media Use
Before engaging with social media, set clear intentions for your time online. Ask yourself what you hope to gain from the experience and be mindful of staying focused on your purpose.

Practicing Digital Detox
Occasionally disconnect from social media and digital devices to recharge and reconnect with the present moment. A digital detox allows you to regain mental clarity and reduce the effects of information overload.

Curating Your Social Media Feed
Mindfully curate your social media feed to include content that aligns with your interests, values, and goals. Unfollow accounts that trigger negative emotions or contribute to information overload.

Limiting Screen Time
Set boundaries for screen time and stick to them. Be intentional about when and how much time you spend on social media or consuming information online.

Embracing Mindful Consumption
Practice mindful consumption of information by critically evaluating its source and relevance. Focus on quality over quantity, and seek information that adds value to your life.

Filtering Information Mindfully
Filter information mindfully to avoid being overwhelmed by unnecessary content. Prioritize what truly matters and let go of information that does not serve your well-being.

Balancing Online and Offline Life
Strive for a healthy balance between online and offline life. Engage in activities that promote well-being, connection, and personal growth beyond the digital realm.

Practicing Self-Compassion
Be kind to yourself and avoid self-criticism if you find it challenging to navigate social media mindfully. Remember that it's a learning process, and every step toward mindfulness is a step in the right direction.

Navigating social media and information overload mindfully is a transformative practice that empowers us to maintain mental clarity, reduce overwhelm, and reclaim control over our digital lives. By setting intentions, curating our online experiences, and practicing mindful consumption, we create a space for meaningful connections and intentional engagement with the digital world. Embrace the power of mindfulness to foster a balanced relationship with technology and information, and discover a renewed sense of well-being and purpose in both the online and offline realms of your life.

CHAPTER 6

Letting Go of Past Hurts and Grudges

Carrying the weight of past hurts and grudges is like burdening ourselves with emotional baggage that hinders our ability to move forward and experience true inner peace. The scars of the past can linger, tainting our present experiences and relationships. However, by embarking on the transformative journey of letting go, we free ourselves from the chains of resentment and find healing and renewal.

In this chapter, we explore the profound impact of holding onto past hurts and grudges. We delve into the emotional toll it takes on our mental well-being and its potential to hinder personal growth and hinder our ability to form healthy connections.

As we navigate through these pages, we delve into the reasons why we hold onto these negative emotions and the misconceptions that keep us trapped in the past. By understanding the psychological dynamics at play, we gain clarity on how to release ourselves from the grip of resentment.

Moreover, we discover the art of forgiveness as a powerful catalyst for healing. Forgiveness is not about condoning hurtful actions or forgetting the past, but rather a deeply liberating act of compassion toward ourselves and others.

Throughout this chapter, we explore strategies for cultivating emotional resilience and building self-compassion. By embracing the practice of letting go, we open ourselves up to a greater sense of inner peace, enhanced emotional well-being, and the potential for more meaningful and harmonious relationships.

As we embark on this journey of releasing past hurts and grudges, we must recognize that it is a process, and it takes courage and self-compassion to navigate. By stepping into the realm of forgiveness and healing, we embark on a path of personal transformation, allowing ourselves to grow, thrive, and embrace a life liberated from the weight of the past.

So, let us turn the page with open hearts and minds, ready to release ourselves from the shackles of past pain. By embracing the power of letting go, we pave the way for a future filled with emotional freedom, resilience, and the capacity to live fully in the present moment.

The Healing Power of Forgiveness and Moving On

Forgiveness is a profound act of liberation that holds the transformative power to heal deep emotional wounds and free us from the chains of resentment. When we hold onto grudges and refuse to forgive, we remain tethered to the past, unable to fully embrace the present or envision a brighter future. Embracing the healing power of forgiveness and moving on is a transformative journey that brings immense emotional and mental well-being.

The Weight of Unforgiveness

Holding onto past hurts and grudges burdens our hearts and minds, affecting our emotional and physical health. It drains our energy, fuels negative emotions, and hinders personal growth.

Understanding Forgiveness

Forgiveness is not condoning hurtful actions or excusing the wrongdoer's behavior. Instead, it is a profound act of compassion and self-love, allowing us to release ourselves from the grip of pain.

Letting Go for Your Own Sake
Forgiveness is not about the other person; it is a gift you give to yourself. By letting go of the past, you liberate yourself from the emotional baggage that hinders your well-being and happiness.

The Misconceptions of Forgiveness
Sometimes, misconceptions about forgiveness hold us back. We may fear that forgiving means we are weak or that we are condoning the hurtful actions. However, forgiveness is an empowering act of strength and self-compassion.

The Art of Self-Compassion
Practicing self-compassion is vital in the journey of forgiveness. We must be gentle with ourselves, acknowledging our pain and emotions without judgment.

The Path to Forgiveness
The path to forgiveness may be challenging, and it is unique for each individual. It involves acknowledging our pain, understanding the impact of the hurt, and choosing to release the resentment.

Healing and Emotional Resilience
Forgiveness is a powerful tool for healing emotional wounds. It allows us to process our emotions and cultivate emotional resilience, enabling us to navigate future challenges with greater strength.

Embracing the Present Moment
By forgiving and letting go, we release ourselves from the grip of the past, enabling us to fully embrace the present moment. This newfound presence enriches our lives and opens us up to new possibilities.

Fostering Meaningful Connections
Forgiveness paves the way for deeper and more meaningful

connections with others. It allows us to form healthier relationships based on trust, empathy, and compassion.

Moving Forward with Renewed Hope
Forgiveness creates a space for personal growth and renewal. It allows us to move forward with hope and optimism, unburdened by the weight of the past.

The healing power of forgiveness and moving on is a transformative journey that leads us to emotional freedom and well-being. By embracing forgiveness, we liberate ourselves from the chains of resentment, cultivate self-compassion, and pave the way for personal growth and meaningful connections. Letting go of past hurts allows us to fully embrace the present and envision a brighter future filled with renewed hope and inner peace. As we embark on this journey of forgiveness, we discover the profound capacity of the human heart to heal and find solace, embracing a life of emotional freedom and resilience.

Releasing Emotional Baggage for a Lighter and Happier Life

Emotional baggage is the accumulation of unresolved emotions, past traumas, and negative experiences that we carry with us throughout life. Just as carrying physical baggage weighs us down, holding onto emotional baggage hinders our ability to lead a lighter and happier life. Releasing emotional baggage is a transformative process that allows us to liberate ourselves from the burdens of the past and create space for greater joy, freedom, and emotional well-being.

Recognizing Emotional Baggage
The first step in releasing emotional baggage is to recognize its presence in our lives. This may involve acknowledging past traumas, unprocessed emotions, and negative thought patterns that continue to affect our daily experiences.

The Impact of Emotional Baggage
Emotional baggage can manifest in various ways, such as anxiety, depression, relationship issues, and self-limiting beliefs. It affects our ability to be present, find joy, and build healthy connections with others.

Accepting Your Emotions
Allow yourself to feel and accept the emotions that arise from your past experiences. Avoid suppressing or judging your feelings, as they are valid and need to be acknowledged for healing to take place.

Seeking Support
Releasing emotional baggage can be a challenging journey, and it's okay to seek support from friends, family, or a professional therapist. Talking to someone can provide clarity, understanding, and guidance in the healing process.

Practicing Self-Compassion
Be gentle and compassionate with yourself as you navigate the process of releasing emotional baggage. Understand that healing takes time, and it's okay to take small steps towards growth and emotional liberation.

Cultivating Forgiveness
Forgiveness is a transformative tool in releasing emotional baggage. It involves forgiving yourself and others for past hurts and choosing to let go of resentment and anger.

Mindful Release
Practice mindfulness as you release emotional baggage. Be present with your emotions, allowing them to arise and pass without judgment or attachment.

Letting Go of Self-Limiting Beliefs
Emotional baggage often feeds into self-limiting beliefs that hold us back. Challenge these beliefs and replace them with affirmations that empower and uplift you.

Creating Healthy Boundaries
Establish healthy boundaries to protect your emotional well-being. Learn to say no to people or situations that drain your energy and trigger old emotional wounds.

Embracing Gratitude and Positivity
Cultivate a gratitude practice and focus on the positive aspects of your life. Shifting your perspective towards gratitude can help counteract the weight of emotional baggage.

Releasing emotional baggage is a transformative journey that leads to a lighter and happier life. By recognizing its presence, accepting your emotions, and seeking support, you can begin the healing process. Practice self-compassion, cultivate forgiveness, and let go of self-limiting beliefs that no longer serve you. Embrace mindfulness and gratitude as you release emotional baggage, creating space for greater joy, emotional freedom, and a renewed sense of well-being. As you liberate yourself from the burdens of the past, you open the door to a brighter and more fulfilling life, filled with resilience, growth, and the capacity to experience true happiness and peace.

Learning from the Past without Dwelling on It

The past holds a treasure trove of experiences, lessons, and memories that shape our journey through life. It is a reservoir of wisdom that can inform our present choices and decisions. Learning from the past is essential for personal growth and self-awareness, but dwelling on it excessively can become a hindrance to our well-being and hinder our ability to fully embrace the present and create a fulfilling future.

Embrace Reflection, Release Regret
Reflection on the past is an invaluable tool for gaining insights into our actions, decisions, and their consequences. However, it is crucial to avoid getting entangled in regrets or lingering on missed opportunities. Instead, focus on the lessons learned and

how you can apply them positively in your present and future endeavors.

Accepting Imperfection and Embracing Growth
Recognize that imperfection is a natural part of the human experience. Mistakes and setbacks are opportunities for growth and learning. Accept them with grace, learn from them, and allow yourself to evolve.

Mindfulness Anchors You in the Present
Practicing mindfulness brings your awareness to the present moment, helping you release attachment to past events and concerns about the future. By living in the present, you experience life more fully and reduce unnecessary worry and anxiety.

Forgiveness Sets You Free
Forgiving yourself and others for past hurts and mistakes is a liberating act of self-compassion. It doesn't mean condoning harmful actions, but rather releasing the emotional burden that comes with holding onto grudges.

Focus on Your Present Goals
While it's essential to learn from the past, it's equally crucial to focus on your present goals and aspirations. Set meaningful intentions and take steps toward creating the future you envision.

Learn from but Don't Repeat the Past
Learning from the past allows you to avoid repeating the same mistakes. Be mindful of patterns and behaviors that might lead you down a familiar, unproductive path, and make conscious choices to avoid them.

Practice Gratitude for the Present
Cultivate gratitude for the experiences and blessings in your life right now. Gratitude shifts your perspective from dwelling on what is lacking to appreciating what you already have.

Seek Support for Healing
If past traumas or unresolved emotions still burden you, seek

support from loved ones or a professional counselor. Healing from the past is a journey that benefits from compassionate guidance.

Release the Need for Approval
Releasing the need for external validation and approval empowers you to make choices based on your values and desires. Freeing yourself from the opinions of others allows you to live authentically.

Create Positive Memories for the Future
While the past shapes you, the present is an opportunity to create positive memories for the future. Engage in experiences that bring you joy, fulfillment, and meaningful connections.

Learning from the past without dwelling on it is a transformative practice that leads to growth, self-awareness, and a sense of empowerment. Embrace reflection while releasing regrets, practice mindfulness to be present in the moment, and forgive to free yourself from the weight of grudges. Focus on your present goals, cultivate gratitude, and seek support for healing when needed. By navigating the balance between learning from the past and living in the present, you pave the way for a brighter, more purposeful future filled with authenticity, contentment, and personal growth.

CHAPTER 7

The Zen of Not Caring

In a world that often demands constant striving for success, approval, and recognition, the concept of "not caring" may seem counterintuitive or even irresponsible. However, at its essence, the Zen of not caring is not about apathy or indifference but about freeing ourselves from the burdens of external expectations and societal pressures. It is a transformative practice that empowers us to focus on what truly matters, find inner peace, and live authentically.

In this chapter, we explore the profound philosophy of not caring and its application in our daily lives. We delve into the misconceptions and stigmas surrounding the idea of detachment and reveal how it can lead us to a more balanced and fulfilling existence.

Throughout these pages, we learn that not caring is not an excuse for complacency or neglecting our responsibilities. Instead, it is about prioritizing our well-being, mental health, and genuine aspirations.

We uncover the liberating power of setting healthy boundaries and releasing ourselves from the weight of external judgments. By doing so, we create space to cultivate self-compassion, authentic connections, and a deeper understanding of ourselves.

Moreover, we explore the harmony of being present in the moment and embracing life as it unfolds, rather than anxiously seeking validation or approval.

As we journey through this chapter, we discover that the Zen of not caring is a path of self-discovery and inner freedom. It encourages us to find our own unique paths, unburdened by society's expectations, and to navigate life with a sense of purpose, intention, and joy.

So, let us embark on this chapter with an open mind and heart, ready to embrace the Zen of not caring. Let us shed the layers of unnecessary worries and expectations, allowing ourselves to rediscover the beauty of simplicity and the profound serenity that comes from living in alignment with our true selves. In the art of not caring, we uncover a transformative philosophy that allows us to embrace life fully, unapologetically, and with a newfound sense of peace and contentment.

Embracing the Philosophy of Detachment and Non-Attachment

In a world filled with attachments to material possessions, relationships, and outcomes, the philosophy of detachment and non-attachment offers a refreshing perspective on living a more liberated and fulfilling life. Rooted in ancient wisdom from various spiritual and philosophical traditions, this philosophy encourages us to free ourselves from the grasping and clinging that often lead to suffering. Embracing detachment and non-attachment is a transformative journey that empowers us to find inner peace, contentment, and a deeper connection to ourselves and the world around us.

Understanding Detachment and Non-Attachment
Detachment is the practice of letting go of our attachments to things, people, and situations. Non-attachment goes a step

further, emphasizing the ability to remain equanimous and unswayed by the inevitable changes and impermanence of life.

Embracing Impermanence

Recognize that everything in life is impermanent, and change is the natural order of the universe. Embracing impermanence allows us to adapt to life's ever-changing nature without resistance.

Relinquishing Control

Detachment and non-attachment involve surrendering the need for control over outcomes. Instead, focus on doing your best in every situation without getting attached to specific results.

Cultivating Inner Peace

As you let go of attachments, you free yourself from the emotional turbulence caused by desires and expectations. Cultivating inner peace becomes possible as you release the need to constantly chase after external validation or approval.

Living in the Present Moment

Detachment and non-attachment anchor you in the present moment. By letting go of regrets about the past and worries about the future, you can fully immerse yourself in the richness of the present.

Finding Freedom from Suffering

Attachment often gives rise to suffering when things don't go as planned. By embracing non-attachment, you release the bonds that tie you to suffering and open the door to greater happiness and contentment.

Practicing Mindfulness

Mindfulness is an essential tool for cultivating detachment and non-attachment. Being mindful allows you to observe your thoughts, emotions, and desires without getting entangled in them.

Nurturing Self-Compassion

As you embrace detachment and non-attachment, be compassionate with yourself. Acknowledge that this is a journey, and it's okay to experience moments of difficulty or attachment. Treat yourself with kindness and gentleness along the way.

Creating Space for Growth
Detachment and non-attachment create space for personal growth and self-discovery. Letting go of attachments allows new experiences and opportunities to unfold without being confined by past conditioning.

Connecting with Interconnectedness
By releasing our narrow focus on individual desires, we begin to recognize our interconnectedness with all beings and the natural world. Non-attachment fosters a sense of unity and compassion for others.

Embracing the philosophy of detachment and non-attachment is a profound journey toward inner freedom and wisdom. By understanding impermanence, relinquishing control, and cultivating inner peace, you liberate yourself from the chains of attachment. Practice mindfulness, nurture self-compassion, and create space for growth and self-discovery. As you let go of the need to grasp and cling, you open yourself to a deeper connection with the present moment and a more profound sense of interconnectedness with all of life. Embrace the philosophy of detachment and non-attachment, and you will find a path to greater fulfillment, contentment, and spiritual awakening.

Practicing Mindfulness and Living in the Present Moment

In our fast-paced and digitally connected world, the present moment often gets overshadowed by worries about the future or regrets about the past. Practicing mindfulness and living in the present moment is a transformative approach that allows us to reclaim our attention, connect with our inner selves, and find peace amidst life's chaos. By embracing mindfulness, we can cultivate a deeper sense of gratitude, contentment, and a profound appreciation for the beauty of each passing moment.

What is Mindfulness?
Mindfulness is the art of being fully present and aware of our thoughts, emotions, and sensations without judgment. It involves observing our experiences with an open and non-reactive mindset.

Reconnecting with the Present
Living in the present moment requires intentional effort. We can start by gently bringing our focus back to the present whenever our minds wander into thoughts of the past or future.

Mindful Breathing and Grounding Techniques
One of the simplest ways to practice mindfulness is through mindful breathing. Pay attention to each breath, feeling the sensation of air entering and leaving your body. Grounding techniques, such as feeling your feet on the ground, can also anchor you in the present moment.

Letting Go of Distractions
The modern world is filled with distractions that pull us away from the present moment. Practice setting aside time to disconnect from technology and embrace moments of stillness and introspection.

Acceptance and Non-Judgment
Mindfulness involves accepting the present moment as it is, without judgment or attachment. Acknowledge your thoughts and emotions without labeling them as good or bad.

Savoring Life's Simple Pleasures
Living in the present allows us to savor life's simple pleasures. Whether it's the taste of a delicious meal, the warmth of the sun on our skin, or the joy of connecting with loved ones, mindfulness enhances our ability to appreciate these experiences fully.

Reducing Stress and Anxiety
Mindfulness has been shown to reduce stress and anxiety by redirecting our attention away from worries and fears. By being present, we focus on what we can control and release the burden of what lies beyond our influence.

Improving Focus and Productivity
With regular mindfulness practice, we sharpen our focus and become more attentive to tasks at hand. This increased concentration enhances our productivity and efficiency.

Enhancing Emotional Regulation
Mindfulness helps us observe our emotions without immediately reacting to them. By creating this space, we can respond to challenging situations with greater clarity and compassion.

Cultivating Gratitude and Contentment
Practicing mindfulness fosters a deeper sense of gratitude for the present moment and the abundance of blessings in our lives. It nurtures contentment by reminding us of the richness in simplicity.

Practicing mindfulness and living in the present moment is a gift we can offer ourselves amidst the demands of modern life. By reconnecting with the present, we find clarity, peace, and a profound connection to ourselves and the world around us. Embrace mindfulness as a daily practice, and let it be the guiding light that illuminates the beauty and wonder of each passing moment. As you cultivate mindfulness, you will discover a richer, more fulfilling existence, grounded in gratitude, serenity, and a deeper understanding of the precious gift of life.

Finding Peace in the Midst of Chaos

Life can be a whirlwind of chaos, with constant demands, challenges, and unexpected twists. Amidst this turbulence, finding inner peace may seem like an elusive goal. However, the ability to find peace is not dependent on external circumstances but lies within each of us. Embracing practices and attitudes that cultivate peace can empower us to navigate through life's storms with grace, resilience, and a sense of calm.

Embrace Mindfulness

Mindfulness is a powerful tool to find peace in the midst of chaos. By grounding ourselves in the present moment, we release the anxieties of the past and the worries about the future. Mindfulness allows us to acknowledge the chaos without becoming overwhelmed by it.

Cultivate Gratitude

Gratitude shifts our focus from what is lacking to what we already have. Amidst chaos, take a moment to appreciate the simple blessings in life. Cultivating gratitude nurtures a sense of contentment and peace.

Create Calming Rituals

Establishing calming rituals in your daily routine can help you find peace amidst chaos. Whether it's a few minutes of meditation, deep breathing exercises, or spending time in nature, these rituals offer a sanctuary of tranquility.

Practice Self-Compassion

In chaotic times, be kind to yourself. Practice self-compassion and avoid self-criticism. Understand that it is okay to feel overwhelmed at times, and allow yourself the space to process emotions.

Set Boundaries

In chaotic situations, setting boundaries is essential. Learn to say no to additional responsibilities when you are already stretched thin. Prioritize self-care and protect your well-being.

Release the Need for Control

Accept that some things are beyond your control. Release the need to micromanage every aspect of your life. Embracing the flow of life with openness allows peace to flourish.

Engage in Activities that Bring Joy

Amidst chaos, make time for activities that bring you joy and rejuvenate your spirit. Engaging in hobbies, spending time with loved ones, or pursuing creative outlets can uplift your mood and foster inner peace.

Limit Exposure to Negative Influences

In chaotic times, be mindful of the information and people you surround yourself with. Limit exposure to negative influences that drain your energy and contribute to the chaos.

Practice Patience

Cultivate patience in the face of uncertainty. Understand that chaotic situations often take time to resolve, and patience allows you to navigate through them with a steady mind.

Seek Solace in Nature

Nature has a calming effect on the mind and soul. Spend time in natural settings, whether it's a park, a beach, or a forest. Nature's serenity can help you find peace amidst chaos.

Finding peace in the midst of chaos is a transformative journey that centers on inner resilience and serenity. Embrace mindfulness, gratitude, and self-compassion as powerful tools. Create calming rituals and set boundaries to protect your well-being. Release the need for control and practice patience. Engage in activities that bring joy and seek solace in the tranquility of nature. As you cultivate these practices and attitudes, you will discover an enduring peace that transcends external circumstances, empowering you to navigate life's chaos with strength, grace, and a profound sense of inner harmony.

CHAPTER 8

Nurturing Self-Love and Self-Worth

In a world that often emphasizes achievement, comparison, and external validation, the practice of self-love and nurturing self-worth becomes a transformative and empowering journey. Embracing these principles is not about arrogance or selfishness but about recognizing our inherent value and treating ourselves with the same kindness and compassion we extend to others.

In this chapter, we embark on a path of self-discovery and self-acceptance, exploring the profound significance of self-love and self-worth in our lives. We delve into the misconceptions and challenges that may hinder our ability to embrace these concepts fully, and we reveal the profound impact that cultivating self-love can have on our well-being, relationships, and overall happiness.

Throughout these pages, we learn that self-love is not a destination but a continuous journey of growth, healing, and self-awareness. It involves celebrating our strengths, accepting our imperfections, and recognizing our inherent worthiness as individuals. Nurturing self-worth means freeing ourselves from the shackles of self-doubt and learning to value ourselves for who we are, not just for what we do or achieve.

As we delve into this chapter, we discover that self-love and self-worth are the foundation for building authentic connections, setting healthy boundaries, and fostering a deep sense of contentment and fulfillment. By cultivating a loving and compassionate relationship with ourselves, we are better equipped to navigate life's challenges, embrace our unique journey, and empower ourselves to live authentically.

So, let us embark on this transformative journey of self-love and self-worth, with open hearts and minds, ready to embrace our true selves with kindness, acceptance, and grace. As we nurture self-love and self-worth, we unlock the keys to a life filled with inner strength, resilience, and a profound appreciation for the remarkable individuals we are meant to be.

The Role of Self-Love in Cultivating a Healthy Perspective

Self-love is a fundamental pillar in developing a healthy and balanced perspective on life and ourselves. It is the foundation upon which we build a positive and compassionate relationship with ourselves, influencing how we perceive the world around us and our place in it. Cultivating self-love is not a selfish act; rather, it is a transformative practice that empowers us to see ourselves and others through a lens of understanding, acceptance, and kindness.

Building Inner Resilience
Self-love nurtures inner resilience, enabling us to bounce back from setbacks and challenges with a sense of self-assurance. When we love and care for ourselves deeply, we are better equipped to face adversity, knowing that we have the strength to overcome obstacles.

Embracing Imperfection
Self-love allows us to embrace our imperfections and vulnerabilities without harsh self-judgment. Rather than seeking perfection, we recognize that being human means having flaws,

and that is what makes us unique and beautiful.

Setting Healthy Boundaries
Loving ourselves empowers us to set healthy boundaries in our relationships. We learn to prioritize our well-being and protect ourselves from harmful influences, fostering a balanced and respectful dynamic with others.

Cultivating Gratitude
Through self-love, we develop a deeper sense of gratitude for the person we are and the life we have. Gratitude helps us see the abundance and beauty around us, even amidst challenges, enhancing our overall perspective on life.

Empathy and Compassion
When we practice self-love, we naturally extend empathy and compassion to others. Understanding and accepting our own vulnerabilities allows us to relate to the struggles and experiences of others with greater empathy and kindness.

Embracing Positive Self-Talk
Self-love transforms our internal dialogue from self-criticism to self-encouragement. By nurturing a positive self-talk, we build a healthier perspective on our abilities and potential.

Reducing Comparison and Envy
Self-love helps us to celebrate our unique qualities without falling into the trap of constant comparison with others. We appreciate our journey and avoid being consumed by envy or jealousy.

Embracing Life's Changes
With self-love, we approach life's changes and transitions with greater acceptance and adaptability. We recognize that change is a natural part of life and approach it with grace and openness.

Encouraging Growth and Self-Development
Loving ourselves inspires us to invest in self-development and personal growth. We believe in our potential and are willing to explore new opportunities and challenges.

Fostering Positive Relationships
Self-love is the cornerstone of healthy relationships. When we love and value ourselves, we attract and nurture positive and supportive connections with others.

Self-love plays a vital role in cultivating a healthy perspective, both towards ourselves and the world around us. It empowers us to build resilience, embrace imperfection, and set healthy boundaries. Through self-love, we develop gratitude, empathy, and a positive self-talk that shapes our outlook on life. By loving ourselves, we foster a deeper connection with others, celebrate individuality, and navigate life's changes with grace and adaptability. Embrace the transformative power of self-love, and you will uncover a healthier, more compassionate perspective that enriches your life and the lives of those around you.

Recognizing Your Inherent Value
Beyond External Validation

In a world where external validation often dominates our perception of self-worth, it is crucial to recognize that our true value extends far beyond the opinions and judgments of others. Embracing our inherent worth is a transformative practice that empowers us to stand firm in our uniqueness, irrespective of external influences. It involves looking within, acknowledging our strengths, embracing our imperfections, and celebrating the essence of who we are.

Understanding Inherent Value
Inherent value is the intrinsic worth that each individual possesses simply by virtue of existing. It is not contingent on achievements, possessions, or approval from others. Recognizing this innate value is the first step towards breaking free from the need for constant external validation.

Embracing Uniqueness

Each of us is a tapestry of experiences, qualities, and perspectives that make us unique. Embrace your individuality and appreciate the diversity you bring to the world. Our differences are what make the human experience rich and beautiful.

Celebrating Your Strengths

Take time to acknowledge and celebrate your strengths, talents, and accomplishments. By recognizing your abilities, you reinforce your belief in your own worth and potential.

Accepting Imperfections

Perfection is an unattainable ideal, and accepting our imperfections is a part of being human. Embrace your flaws and see them as opportunities for growth and learning.

Releasing the Need for Approval

Seeking constant approval from others can be a never-ending pursuit. Free yourself from this cycle by trusting your judgment and decisions. Remember that your worth does not diminish based on the opinions of others.

Validating Yourself from Within

Look within yourself for validation and affirmation. Practice self-compassion and self-appreciation. Understand that you are deserving of love and kindness, both from yourself and others.

Nurturing Self-Love

Cultivate a deep sense of self-love and care. Treat yourself with the same tenderness and consideration you would offer a beloved friend. Nurture a positive and compassionate relationship with yourself.

Setting Authentic Goals

Instead of chasing external achievements to validate your worth, set authentic goals that align with your passions and values. Focus on personal growth and fulfillment rather than seeking validation from others.

Practicing Gratitude

Gratitude helps shift our focus from what we lack to what we already have. Be grateful for the unique qualities and opportunities you possess. Gratitude reinforces your inherent value.

Surrounding Yourself with Supportive People
Surround yourself with people who appreciate and uplift you for who you are. Seek out relationships that nurture your sense of self-worth and encourage personal growth.

Recognizing your inherent value beyond external validation is a liberating journey of self-discovery and self-acceptance. Embrace your uniqueness, celebrate your strengths, and accept your imperfections. Release the need for constant approval and seek validation from within. Nourish self-love, practice gratitude, and set authentic goals aligned with your passions. Surround yourself with supportive relationships that uplift and appreciate you. As you internalize your inherent value, you will find a profound sense of empowerment and contentment that no external validation can match. Embrace the realization that your worth extends far beyond the judgments of others, and you will discover a wellspring of confidence, strength, and authenticity within yourself.

Self-Care Practices to Boost Your Self-Esteem

Self-esteem is the foundation of a healthy and positive relationship with oneself. Engaging in regular self-care practices is a powerful way to nurture and elevate self-esteem. By investing time and effort into caring for your physical, emotional, and mental well-being, you reinforce your sense of self-worth and cultivate a deeper appreciation for who you are. Here are some self-care practices that can boost your self-esteem:

Practice Self-Compassion
Treat yourself with the same kindness and understanding you would offer to a friend. When faced with challenges or mistakes,

practice self-compassion instead of harsh self-criticism.

Prioritize Your Needs
Make your well-being a priority. Set aside time for activities that bring you joy, relaxation, and fulfillment. Putting yourself first when needed is not selfish; it is an essential aspect of self-care.

Establish Healthy Boundaries
Respect your time, energy, and emotional well-being by setting healthy boundaries with others. Learn to say no to commitments or relationships that drain you and prioritize those that uplift and support you.

Celebrate Your Achievements
Acknowledge and celebrate your accomplishments, both big and small. Take pride in your successes and use them as reminders of your capabilities and strengths.

Engage in Physical Activity
Regular exercise has numerous benefits for both physical and mental well-being. Engaging in physical activities you enjoy boosts your mood, reduces stress, and enhances your self-esteem.

Practice Mindfulness and Self-Reflection
Engage in mindfulness practices, such as meditation or journaling, to connect with your inner self. Self-reflection fosters self-awareness and helps you understand your thoughts, emotions, and desires.

Surround Yourself with Positive Influences
Surround yourself with people who uplift and support you. Build a network of positive influences that celebrate your uniqueness and encourage your growth.

Challenge Negative Self-Talk
Become aware of negative self-talk and actively challenge it. Replace self-limiting beliefs with positive affirmations that reinforce your self-worth.

Take Care of Your Physical Appearance
While appearance is not the sole measure of self-esteem, taking care of your personal hygiene and grooming can boost your confidence and how you feel about yourself.

Engage in Activities You Love
Make time for hobbies and activities that bring you joy and fulfillment. Engaging in pursuits you love reinforces your self-confidence and reminds you of your passions and interests.

Seek Support and Professional Help if Needed
If you struggle with low self-esteem, consider seeking support from friends, family, or a therapist. Professional help can provide guidance in building healthy self-esteem and addressing underlying issues.

Embrace Self-Appreciation
Learn to appreciate your unique qualities and strengths. Recognize that you are worthy and deserving of love and respect simply because you exist.

Self-care practices play a vital role in boosting self-esteem and fostering a positive relationship with yourself. By incorporating these practices into your daily life, you nourish your self-worth, build resilience, and cultivate a deeper appreciation for your true essence. Remember that self-esteem is a journey, and practicing self-care is an ongoing process of self-discovery and growth. Embrace these practices with compassion and dedication, and you will experience a profound transformation in how you perceive yourself and your place in the world.

CONCLUSION

Embrace the Art of Not Caring and Flourish

As we reach the conclusion of "The Art of Not Caring: Embrace Freedom and Inner Peace," we find ourselves standing at the threshold of a profound transformation. Throughout this transformative journey, we have explored the depths of self-discovery, challenged societal norms, and embarked on a path towards authentic living and inner peace. Now, armed with newfound wisdom and empowerment, it is time to take the next steps and embrace the art of not caring to flourish in every aspect of life.

We have learned that not caring does not signify apathy or indifference. Instead, it is an enlightened approach to life, where we free ourselves from the burden of external expectations and societal pressures. By detaching from the need for constant control and validation, we liberate ourselves to embrace our unique selves fully.

Embracing our failures as stepping stones to growth and success, we recognize that life's setbacks do not define us but rather provide invaluable lessons. By practicing self-compassion, we offer ourselves the kindness and understanding that enables us to thrive amidst challenges.

The art of not caring extends beyond our individual selves. We have learned to foster genuine connections with others by embracing authenticity and overcoming the fear of judgment and rejection. Celebrating our uniqueness and appreciating diversity, we release the constant comparison trap and find contentment in what we have.

We have delved into the power of forgiveness and the art of releasing emotional baggage, freeing ourselves from the chains of past hurts and grudges. Through practicing mindfulness and living in the present moment, we find solace amidst chaos and deepen our connection with the beauty of life.

Recognizing our inherent value beyond external validation, we have cultivated self-love and boosted our self-esteem through self-care practices. By setting healthy boundaries and nurturing our well-being, we empower ourselves to lead lives that align with our passions and values.

As we conclude this transformative journey, let us remember that embracing the art of not caring is a lifelong practice. It is a continual commitment to self-discovery, growth, and self-acceptance. In the face of life's ups and downs, let us draw upon the wisdom and empowerment gained from this journey to navigate with grace and resilience.

May this book serve as a guiding light, illuminating the path towards authentic living, inner freedom, and profound peace. May we find the courage to stand firm in our uniqueness, celebrate ourselves and others, and cultivate a world where self-compassion and authenticity flourish.

Embrace the art of not caring, and you will discover a life filled with joy, contentment, and a profound sense of inner liberation. Flourish in your journey, for you are the artist of your life, creating a masterpiece that reflects the beauty of your true self.

Thank you for accompanying us on this transformative journey.

May your life be enriched with the freedom to be unapologetically yourself and the inner peace that arises from embracing the art of not caring. Go forth and flourish with the profound wisdom and empowerment gained from this exploration. The world awaits your authentic self.

Made in the USA
Middletown, DE
21 December 2023